STUDY JOURNAL

FOR

THE FIVE DYSFUNCTIONS OF A TEAM

BY PATRICK LENCIONI

BlinkRead

THIS BOOK REVIEW LOG BOOK BELONGS TO :

HOW TO USE THIS JOURNAL:

This book has been uniquely prepared for either personal use or to be used in a group study and it provides a safe space for you to freely express yourself without being judged by others. Using this journal in a group study is completely up to you.

The approaches in this journal are meant to help everyone irrespective of your age, race, gender, culture and boundaries, get the best out of the main book.

In order to effectively make use of this journal, you need to have already purchased the main book.

This book and the main text go hand-in-hand. After reading each chapter/section and familiarizing yourself with it, turn to the journal and answer the respective sections.

Try to answer each question to the best of your ability and as truthfully as you possibly can. You can skip some sections and return to them at a

later time if you do not feel ready enough to answer them.

This journal would increase the depth of your knowledge and understanding of the main book.

It is my hope that this book greatly benefits you and positively transforms your life for the best.

In concluding, as a reminder, these are what you need to use journal;

- The main book
- A pen or pencil

WHY YOU NEED THIS COMPANION JOURNAL

Over time, several studies have continued to point out the need and importance for journaling to boost learning, help you reach your goals and improve the quality of your life as you apply lessons from the main book to your real life.

Without commitment and dedication, achieving the goals from the main book is impossible.

With this journal, you can effectively organize your thoughts, make important connections between thoughts, feelings, and behaviours, and reap the full rewards as you enrich your knowledge to discover and rediscover yourself.

Come along on this path of progress as you put in the much-needed conscious effort to accelerate your personal development, stretch your mind and reach your full potential.

In addition, you can set and achieve goals and track your progress each day.

ABOUT PATRICK LENCIONI

Patrick Lencioni is an American writer of books on business management, particularly about team management. He is the founder and president of The Table Group, a management consulting firm specializing in executive team development and organizational health. As a consultant and keynote speaker, he has worked with thousands of senior executives and their teams. Patrick has supported organizations ranging from Fortune 500 companies and high-tech startups to universities and nonprofits. Lencioni is the author of 11 best-selling books, including The Advantage and The Ideal Team Player.

INTRODUCTION

The Five Dysfunctions of a Team is a fable-based story of Kathryn Petersen, the new CEO of DecisionTech. She joins a company that has a more experienced and talented executive team than any of its competitors. They have more cash, better technology, and a more powerful Board of Directors. That said, they are behind their competitors in terms of both revenue and customer growth. After meeting with the Board, Executive Team, and staff, she identifies the team's dysfunctions.

StoryShot #1: Trust Is the Foundation of Success

Lencioni outlines that an absence of trust is the most significant barrier to team success. Trust and loyalty are an integral part of any team. Just imagine how violent gangs require their new members to kill to establish trust and loyalty. In more professional environments, trust allows team members to feel comfortable in accepting their weaknesses and vulnerabilities. So, without trust, it is unlikely that team members will bring innovative ideas or challenge authority. Both of these are required for considerable improvement to occur. Lencioni concludes that a team without trust is merely a group of people who feel they need to be right and aren't willing to take any risks.

Trust is also crucial for effective teamwork. Trust allows team members to communicate healthily and openly. They are then better equipped to solve complex solutions far quicker. Instead of beating around the bush, the team gets straight to the issue at hand. Without trust, these issues will be left undiscussed and decisions will only include a select few's opinions.

In this book, Lencioni uses the departure of DecisionTech's head of sales as an example of how trust can encourage open communication. Carlos Amador, the head of customer support, suggested he took the position. But, the rest of the team felt that other team members had more experience and were more suitable for the role. As the team had a foundation of trust, they all felt comfortable voicing their opinion to Carlos and the rest of the team. Carlos was not offended because he respected his team members' opinions. So, the team made the correct decision of hiring the chief operations officer for the post. Without trust, the team would not have challenged Carlos' suggestion, and they arguably would have been less efficient.

StoryShot #2: Avoid Deliberately Fostering Mistrust
Some businesses actively allow their executive team members to have a culture of mistrust. These companies mistakenly assume they can produce better results by

introducing this culture. A large newspaper chain introduced this approach by pitting prominent team members against each other. In general, a newspaper chain will arrange three executive team members to announce an early promotion and the three invitees are precursors to the work. The CEO believed that encouraging these managers to compete would produce the organization's best results as each manager would work hard to prove themselves. By doing this, the CEO emphasizes the performance of the three divisions rather than the whole business. Such a scenario normally begins with a bitter competition between the three bosses. The bosses won't cooperate so that they can push others out of control. And while the divisions of these executives may display excellent results, the whole organization's results could be compromised.

StoryShot #3: How You Can Build Trust

Trust is built upon vulnerability. The modern business world is hyper-focused on competitiveness and protecting your own interests. Lencioni explains that you have to challenge some of these views to build a team that incorporates trust. For example, team members should always own up when they have made a mistake. Doing this will normalize talking about mistakes and learning from them. This will be better for individual team members and the team as a whole.

Lencioni recommends specific trust-building exercises. For example, simply sitting in a circle and telling each other about their childhoods and where they grew up. This base-level knowledge of other employees is enough to leave employees more at ease. Building on this, he also suggests you get your team to take turns openly acknowledging a weakness they possess that could limit the team's potential. But, this weakness should be followed by a strength they possess that could push the team towards success. When you and your teammates are transparent about your faults, you take down the veil of perfection and allow open and honest feedback to find its way into team discussions. This leads to another point made by Lencioni, which is that everyone's performance should be transparent.

StoryShot #4: Peer-to-Peer Accountability Requires Transparent Performance

Accepting mistakes relies on your team becoming transparent regarding performance. Transparency reduces the awkwardness associated with pointing out that a team member is under-performing. Without transparency, this claim is not backed by evidence. With transparency, all will see that they need to improve. Being able to identify who is under-performing will allow your team to be more effective in meeting deadlines, improving results, and increasing efficiency.

Transparency also encourages peer-to-peer accountability. This is crucial, as it prevents the team leader from being burdened as the sole source of discipline. Teams often avoid accountability as they worry it will ruin personal relationships. Lencioni explains that a lack of accountability leads to resentment of under-performers and disciplinarians. So, the relationships are less healthy when a team is lacking accountability. Accountable teams can improve their relationships because they develop respect when others adhere to the same high standards. Finally, accountability allows team members to see personal improvements as critical in working toward a common good rather than a personal attack.

StoryShot #5: Fear of Conflict

Conflict avoidance is one of the most frequent dysfunctions within business teams. Team members avoid conflict, and other team members aim to stop conflicts when they arise. Lencioni outlines that debates can be extremely effective if the team is based on trust. Your team is more likely to reach the optimal decision if people disagree. Having a team consisting of people telling you what you want to hear will not be as effective as possible. A mixture of opinions and experiences is crucial for making good decisions. Lencioni describes conflict as the heart of innovation and progress. Nobody identified innovative ideas by agreeing with the status quo.

Some examples of constructive conflict within the workplace would be debating company behaviors, processes, services and products. You should always avoid conflicts that are based on personal attacks. At their heart, these conflicts are not productive and will not improve your team's likelihood of success. So, try to encourage healthy conflict in meetings by creating a team management charter. This charter can promote candid and passionate debate. Then, have every team member sign this charter and bring it to every meeting. Conflict will actually make team members enjoy meetings more. Conflict is interesting and this is why Lencioni compares meetings to the entertainment of watching a movie.

Again, trust is the foundation of overcoming the dysfunctions observed in teams. Trust is crucial for identifying the best possible solutions to any challenges. It also enables conflict because team members who trust each other will be comfortable even when engaging in a passionate and emotional debate over a tricky issue.

StoryShot #6: Lack of Commitment

Sitting on the fence is what will make your team fail. Commitment is fundamental to success. One of the key traits of great teams is they can make decisions and then stand by them. This is because they know that any decision is better than no decision, especially when it comes to important ones. Your team needs to commit to a strategy. Conflict is fundamental to identifying the best strategy. After you have decided upon a strategy, every team member must be on board. So, even those who disagree with the decision must be fully committed. Importantly, productive conflict often allows people to be better committed to decisions, even if they disagree. Great teams understand consensus to mean that everyone is committed and understands the greater goal, even if the decision made is not the one they voiced. Suppose a person's opinions and thoughts are not properly discussed. They are less likely to commit to an alternative opinion. A lack of commitment will make it impossible to achieve a consensus among a team, leading to disinterest, resentment, and stagnation.

Leaders can help develop this commitment by encouraging each team member to contribute to every discussion. The leader must promote this open exchange over and over again until it becomes accepted. Once the atmosphere is one of agreeing to disagree, real progress is not far behind. By reviewing team decisions after every meeting and defining roles and deadlines, the leader can focus on ongoing commitments.

StoryShot #7: Accountability Relies on Commitment

Healthy teams assign accountability and hold their members accountable. They also help them when things slip.

Without team commitment, team members will always avoid accountability. Team members who commit to an idea or decision do it because they feel their input matters and expect to be held accountable. If their input seems unimportant, they feel they aren't responsible for the results. This lack of accountability in the individual will always weaken the accountability of the team.

StoryShot #8: Inattention to Results

Inattention to results can easily creep into a team when they have too many priorities to focus on. None of the priorities are then completed to a high standard. Instead, teams need to always be focused on what matters, which is the results. Until the desired results are agreed upon by the whole team, nothing worthy will ever happen. This is partly because team members cannot be accountable if there are no results set as goals. With accountability in place, team focuses naturally on results which creates a tighter bond among team members. The leader ensures the desired results are clear and that final results are shared and rewarded in a team setting.

StoryShot #9: Focus on Team Goals Rather Than Individual Goals

Keep the team focused on team results (instead of individual results) by connecting personal rewards to team results. For example, team members only receive an extra day off at the end of the month if they hit their collective monthly target. Team rewards remind team members that if the team doesn't win, no one wins. Great teams consist of team members who understand that team goals must always be prioritized over individual goals.

Individuals who are not willing to put the collective goals above their individual goals have to be removed. These individuals will influence the other team members by making them also forget about their collective goals. So, the team can rapidly lose its competitive edge. Progress will stagnate as team members start worrying about their careers rather than team performance.

Lencioni outlines how effective team goals encourage collective rather than individual motivation. You need to produce team goals that are clearly defined and easy to measure. These goals will prevent team members from interpreting the team goals through their own lens. So, it will be harder for team members to avoid these team goals in favor of their individual goals.

StoryShot #10: Team Cohesion Improves Results

All great teams are stronger than the sum of their parts. You want to create a team where individuals are more effective as part of the team rather than individually. Some teams are filled with talented individuals but struggle to work together. These teams will be wasting time and energy on business politics. They will try to outshine their fellow team members, which will only impact the collective team performance. It will also encourage strong team members to leave due to the poor company culture.

StoryShot #11: Great Teams Spend a Lot of Time Together

Lencioni encourages teams to meet regularly so that they can become more in-sync with each other. Meeting regularly will allow team members to build a strong rapport and trust. So, they will be better equipped to quickly and effectively resolve any personal issues. These personal issues and conflicts are also better dealt with face-to-face. This means having your team situated within the same working space is an important decision to make. Finally, face-to-face meetings allow team members to have better insight into what they do within the team. There is less risk of redundant work being produced or miscommunications occurring. For example, strong rapport reduces the chances of overlapping work creeping into your team. It also allows resources to be allocated to the best-suited individuals.

Final StoryShots Review and Analysis

The Five Dysfunctions of a Team offers advice for how small businesses can outperform businesses that are throwing considerable money into their organization. The key to doing so is tackling the five dysfunctions, which are:

Absence of trust — Unwilling to be vulnerable within the group.

Fear of conflict — Seeking artificial harmony over constructive passionate debate.

Lack of commitment — Feigning buy-in for group decisions creates ambiguity throughout the organization.

Avoidance of accountability — Ducking the responsibility to call peers, superiors on counterproductive behavior which sets low standards

In attention to results — Focusing on personal success, status and ego before team success.

ACTIVITIES

Journal down Your Thoughts in Real-Time as you Read the
Main book.

My Thoughts

Other books I want to read because of this book

CHAPTER NO: _____

My Thoughts

Other books I want to read because of this book

My Thoughts

Other books I want to read because of this book

ly Thoughts

Other books I want to read because of this book

My Thoughts

Other books I want to read because of this book

y Thoughts

ther books I want to read because of this book

My Thoughts

Other books I want to read because of this book

My Thoughts

Other books I want to read because of this book

My Thoughts

Other books I want to read because of this book

My Thoughts

Other books I want to read because of this book

My Thoughts

Other books I want to read because of this book

y Thoughts

ther books I want to read because of this book

My Thoughts

Other books I want to read because of this book

CHAPTER NO: _______

My Thoughts

Other books I want to read because of this book

My Thoughts

Other books I want to read because of this book

CHAPTER NO: _____

My Thoughts

Other books I want to read because of this book

My Thoughts

Other books I want to read because of this book

y Thoughts

ther books I want to read because of this book

My Thoughts

Other books I want to read because of this book

CHAPTER NO: _____

My Thoughts

Other books I want to read because of this book

My Thoughts

Other books I want to read because of this book

y Thoughts

_____

_____

_____

_____

_____

_____

_____

_____

_____

_____

_____

_____

_____

_____

_____

_____

_____

_____

Other books I want to read because of this book

My Thoughts

Other books I want to read because of this book

y Thoughts

ther books I want to read because of this book

My Thoughts

Other books I want to read because of this book

CHAPTER NO: _____

My Thoughts

Other books I want to read because of this book

My Thoughts

Other books I want to read because of this book

CHAPTER NO: ________

ly Thoughts

Other books I want to read because of this book

My Thoughts

Other books I want to read because of this book

y Thoughts

ther books I want to read because of this book

My Thoughts

Other books I want to read because of this book

My Thoughts

Other books I want to read because of this book

CHAPTER NO: ________

My Thoughts

Other books I want to read because of this book

CHAPTER NO: _____

My Thoughts

Other books I want to read because of this book

My Thoughts

Other books I want to read because of this book

y Thoughts

ther books I want to read because of this book

CHAPTER NO: _____

My Thoughts

Other books I want to read because of this book

CHAPTER NO: _____

My Thoughts

Other books I want to read because of this book

My Thoughts

Other books I want to read because of this book

CHAPTER NO: _____

My Thoughts

Other books I want to read because of this book

My Thoughts

Other books I want to read because of this book

ly Thoughts

Other books I want to read because of this book

My Thoughts

Other books I want to read because of this book

CHAPTER NO: ________

My Thoughts

Other books I want to read because of this book

My Thoughts

Other books I want to read because of this book

CHAPTER NO: _____

My Thoughts

Other books I want to read because of this book

My Thoughts

Other books I want to read because of this book

My Thoughts

Other books I want to read because of this book

CHAPTER NO: _____

My Thoughts

Other books I want to read because of this book

My Thoughts

Other books I want to read because of this book

My Thoughts

Other books I want to read because of this book

My Thoughts

Other books I want to read because of this book

My Thoughts

Other books I want to read because of this book

y Thoughts

ther books I want to read because of this book

CHAPTER NO: _____

My Thoughts

Other books I want to read because of this book

My Thoughts

Other books I want to read because of this book

CHAPTER NO: _____

My Thoughts

Other books I want to read because of this book

My Thoughts

Other books I want to read because of this book

My Thoughts

Other books I want to read because of this book

CHAPTER NO: _____

My Thoughts

Other books I want to read because of this book

My Thoughts

Other books I want to read because of this book

My Thoughts

Other books I want to read because of this book

My Thoughts

Other books I want to read because of this book

My Thoughts

Other books I want to read because of this book

My Thoughts

Other books I want to read because of this book

My Thoughts

Other books I want to read because of this book

My Thoughts

Other books I want to read because of this book

My Thoughts

Other books I want to read because of this book

My Thoughts

Other books I want to read because of this book

My Thoughts

_____

_____

_____

_____

_____

_____

_____

_____

_____

_____

_____

_____

_____

_____

_____

_____

_____

Other books I want to read because of this book

My Thoughts

Other books I want to read because of this book

My Thoughts

Other books I want to read because of this book

My Thoughts

Other books I want to read because of this book

My Thoughts

Other books I want to read because of this book

My Thoughts

Other books I want to read because of this book

My Thoughts

Other books I want to read because of this book

My Thoughts

Other books I want to read because of this book

CHAPTER NO: _______

ly Thoughts

ther books I want to read because of this book

My Thoughts

Other books I want to read because of this book

My Thoughts

Other books I want to read because of this book

My Thoughts

Other books I want to read because of this book

CHAPTER NO: _____

My Thoughts

Other books I want to read because of this book

My Thoughts

Other books I want to read because of this book

My Thoughts

Other books I want to read because of this book

My Thoughts

Other books I want to read because of this book

My Thoughts

Other books I want to read because of this book

My Thoughts

Other books I want to read because of this book

My Thoughts

Other books I want to read because of this book

My Thoughts

_____
_____
_____
_____
_____
_____
_____
_____
_____
_____
_____
_____
_____
_____
_____
_____
_____
_____
_____

Other books I want to read because of this book

CHAPTER NO: _____

My Thoughts

Other books I want to read because of this book

My Thoughts

Other books I want to read because of this book

My Thoughts

Other books I want to read because of this book

My Thoughts

Other books I want to read because of this book

My Thoughts

_____

_____

_____

_____

_____

_____

_____

_____

_____

_____

_____

_____

_____

_____

_____

Other books I want to read because of this book

My Thoughts

Other books I want to read because of this book

Printed in Great Britain
by Amazon

65677042R00068